Complete NuWave Cookbook

50 Amazingly Easy
to Fry, Bake, Grill and Roast Low-Fat Meals
in 30 Minutes or Less

Sara Parker

Text Copyright © Sara Parker

Legal & Disclaimer

The information contained in this book and its contents is not designed to replace or take the place of any form of medical or professional advice; and is not meant to replace the need for independent medical, financial, legal or other professional advice or services, as may be required. The content and information in this book has been provided for educational and entertainment purposes only.

The content and information contained in this book has been compiled from sources deemed reliable, and it is accurate to the best of the Author's knowledge, information and belief. However, the Author cannot guarantee its accuracy and validity and cannot be held liable for any errors and/or omissions. Further, changes are periodically made to this book as and when needed. Where appropriate and/or necessary, you must consult a professional (including but not limited to your doctor, attorney, financial advisor or such other professional advisor) before using any of the suggested remedies, techniques, or information in this book.

Table of Contents

Introduction

First of all I want to thank you for buying my book. I have gathered all my experience in cooking there. This cookbook contains the most delicious and useful Nuwave Oven Recipes that you can only find.

Thanks to the Nuwave Cookbook you can enjoy your favorite dishes with almost no fat and low calories. Thanks to a special technology a lot of fat from the food goes away while cooking and you get the same favorite dishes you like, but with a low fat content.

Because of these unique features, the Nuwave oven is becoming very popular in the kitchens of most Americans, gradually replacing the traditional frying stoves. Now you can easily cook your favorite meat loaves, juicy pork or roast beef, fry chicken wings or French fries. And all with a minimum of fat and calories.

This cookbook will provide you with a large number of recipes that have been specially developed for the Nuwave oven. And when you figure out how to cook in this unique oven, you can adapt even more fried recipes and cook literally whatever you want.

Don't deny yourself the pleasure of preparing succulent and aromatic meat dishes for you and your family. Turn on your Nuwave oven and let's get started!

How Does NuWave Oven Work?

Nuwave Oven presents a brand new way of cooking. This oven uses 3 different temperatures together:

- **Conduction** - is a type of cooking that uses the heat transferred from the hot materials to the materials it comes into contact with. This is how we usually cook using a frying pan. The food is placed on something hot and cooked in this way.
- **Convection** – is an old method of cooking that uses circulating hot air to cook food. Nuwave Oven uses a quiet motor and a specially designed fan to ensure that the hot air inside the oven is evenly distributed over food.
- **Infrared** – is a special kind of heat produced by infrared rays. Nuwave uses a patented technology that allows food to be cooked well from the inside and looks great on the outside.

Thus, by combining all three effective cooking methods, Nuwave Oven prepares your favourite dishes much faster and more efficiently than other cooking methods. This oven is particularly effective for meat dishes as well as frozen foods, as it does not require additional defrosting.

Benefits of NuWave Oven

Nuwave is a really new way of cooking. By using three cooking methods at once, you can cook more efficiently. But it's not the only advantage of this kitchen appliance. Below you can find some benefits of Nuwave Oven.

Meat, poultry and seafood meals will become more delicious
Actually, you can cook at Nuwave Oven almost anything from vegetables to poultry. But fish and meat dishes are the most delicious in this oven.

In addition, poultry such as chicken or turkey can also be cooked very deliciously. Special cooking methods allow you to make chicken or turkey very tender and juicy inside, with an incredibly appetizing and crispy crust outside.

Healthy cooking
Three types of temperatures can be used together to remove almost all fat from products. But at the same time your meals remain tasty and juicy.

In addition, thanks to fast cooking, food retains a large number of nutrients. This makes any dish cooked in Nuwave Oven useful and low-fat.

Saving time
One of the main benefits of Nuwave Oven is its ability to save time. Time is a very important resource for a modern people and everyone strives to do everything quickly and efficiently. This also concerns cooking. Just put the food in the oven, adjust the temperature and turn on the device. That's it! Spend your time on more useful things, such as communicating with loved ones or watching a useful program.

Another way to save time is to cook frozen foods without defrosting. Yes, you've read that correctly! You don't have to defrost food to room temperature before you cook it. Just take the frozen food out of the fridge, put it in the oven, set the right temperature and keep doing your job. Your delicious food will be ready soon.

Saving energy

Despite the fact that Nuwave Oven uses three types of heat you won't waste a lot of energy but save it. Wondering how this happens? Then read on.

The thing is that usually in different kitchen appliances pre-heating is used. That is, before you put food in the oven, you need to heat the device to the desired temperature. Using Nuwave Oven, you no longer have to do this. Just put your food in the oven and turn it on - the food will start to cook right away!

These and other benefits make using Nuwave Oven easy, simple and efficient. Try it and you'll see for yourself!

NuWave Oven Temperature Conversion Guide

Oven Temperature in Fahrenheit	Oven Temperature in Celsius	Power Level
106 degrees Fahrenheit	41 degrees Celsius	1
116 degrees Fahrenheit	47 degrees Celsius	2
150 degrees Fahrenheit	66 degrees Celsius	3
175 degrees Fahrenheit	79 degrees Celsius	4
225 degrees Fahrenheit	107 degrees Celsius	5
250 degrees Fahrenheit	121 degrees Celsius	6
275 degrees Fahrenheit	135 degrees Celsius	7
300 degrees Fahrenheit	149 degrees Celsius	8
325 degrees Fahrenheit	163 degrees Celsius	9
342 degrees Fahrenheit	172 degrees Celsius	10 (HI)

Cooking Measurement Conversion Chart

Liquid Measures

1 gal = 4 qt = 8 pt = 16 cups = 128 fl oz
½ gal = 2 qt = 4 pt = 8 cups = 64 fl oz
¼ gal = 1 qt = 2 pt = 4 cups = 32 fl oz
½ qt = 1 pt = 2 cups = 16 fl oz
¼ qt = ½ pt = 1 cup = 8 fl oz

Dry Measures

1 cup = 16 Tbsp = 48 tsp = 250ml
¾ cup = 12 Tbsp = 36 tsp = 175ml
⅔ cup = 10 ⅔ Tbsp = 32 tsp = 150ml
½ cup = 8 Tbsp = 24 tsp = 125ml
⅓ cup = 5 ⅓ Tbsp = 16 tsp = 75ml
¼ cup = 4 Tbsp = 12 tsp = 50ml
⅛ cup = 2 Tbsp = 6 tsp = 30ml
1 Tbsp = 3 tsp = 15ml

Dash or Pinch or Speck = less than ⅛ tsp

Quickies

1 fl oz = 30 ml
1 oz = 28.35 g
1 lb = 16 oz (454 g)
1 kg = 2.2 lb
1 quart = 2 pints

U.S.	Canadian
¼ tsp	1.25 mL
½ tsp	2.5 mL
1 tsp	5 mL
1 Tbl	15 mL
¼ cup	50 mL
⅓ cup	75 mL
½ cup	125 mL
⅔ cup	150 mL
¾ cup	175 mL
1 cup	250 mL
1 quart	1 liter

Recipe Abbreviations

Cup = c or C
Fluid = fl
Gallon = gal
Ounce = oz
Package = pkg
Pint = pt
Pound = lb or #
Quart = qt
Square = sq
Tablespoon = T or Tbl
    or TBSP or TBS
Teaspoon = t or tsp

*Some measurements were rounded

Fahrenheit (°F) to Celcius (°C)

$°C = (°F - 32) × 5/9$

Fahrenheit	Celcius
32°F	0°C
40°F	4°C
140°F	60°C
150°F	65°C
160°F	70°C
225°F	107°C
250°F	121°C
275°F	135°C
300°F	150°C
325°F	165°C
350°F	177°C
375°F	190°C
400°F	205°C
425°F	220°C
450°F	230°C
475°F	245°C
500°F	260°C

OVEN TEMPERATURES

WARMING: 200°F
VERY SLOW: 250°F - 275°F
SLOW: 300°F - 325°F
MODERATE: 350°F - 375°F
HOT: 400°F - 425°F
VERY HOT: 450°F - 475°F

Delicious Morning Recipes

Cinnamon Twists

- Ready in 15 minutes
- Servings: 2

Ingredients

- 10 oz frozen bread sticks
- 2 tbsp brown sugar
- 1 tsp ground cinnamon

Directions

1. In a large mixing bowl combine brown sugar and ground cinnamon. Mix well and transfer the mixture to a shallow bowl.
2. Place a single breadstick in the cinnamon sugar mixture and roll until well coated.
3. Place on a 3-inch rack and bake on 'HI' for about 12 to 14 minutes, flipping it over at the halfway mark.
4. Serve and enjoy.

Nutritional Info

- Calories: 170
- Total Fat: 7g
- Carbs: 26g
- Protein: 1g

Healthy Low-Fat Granola

- Ready in 25 minutes
- Servings: 4

Ingredients

- 2 c. old-fashioned oats
- 2 tbsp flax seed
- 2 tbsp wheat germ
- 2 tbsp coconut flakes
- 2 tbsp pumpkin or sunflower seeds
- 2 tbsp sliced almonds
- 1/3 c. maple syrup
- ¼ c apple juice
- A pinch of ground cinnamon, salt and vanilla

Directions

1. In a large mixing bowl combine all the ingredients. Stir to combine thoroughly.
2. Line rimmed cooking sheet with parchment paper. Spread mixture uniformly on cooking sheet.
3. Place pan in NuWave on 1-inch rack. Cook at 350 degrees at a power level high for 10 minutes. Stir, and cook for an addition 10-15 minutes, until lightly browned.

Nutritional Info

- Calories: 378

- Total Fat: 5.6g
- Carbs: 79.3g
- Protein: 8.5g

Breakfast Ham, Cheese, and Bacon Quiche

- Ready in 25 minutes
- Servings: 4

Ingredients

- Pie crust
- 1 c. ham, diced
- 4 bacon slices
- 1 ½ c. shredded cheddar cheese
- 1 tbsp flour
- 3 large eggs
- 1½ c. skimmed milk
- Salt and ground black pepper to taste

Directions

1. Place pie crust on the 1-inch rack and bake on High power (350 degrees) for 6-7 minutes, until lightly brown. Set aside to chill.
2. Spread ham and bacon evenly across the bottommost of pie crust. Dust cheese evenly on top.
3. Meanwhile in a medium-sized bowl mix together flour, large eggs, milk. season with salt and pepper and stir to combine well. Pour the mixture into the pie crust.
4. Place on 1-inch rack and bake on High power 350°C for 15 minutes. Decrease heat to Power Level 8 (300 degrees F) and cook for an additional 10 minutes or until a toothpick inserted in centre comes out clear. Let quiche sit for 10 minutes before slicing. Serve warm.

Nutritional Info

- Calories: 220
- Total Fat: 7.2g
- Total carbs: 22.6g
- Protein: 15.3g

Nuwave Oven Bacon

- Ready in 10 minutes
- Servings: 4

Ingredients

- 8 slices bacon
- 4 slices bread

Directions

1. Line bottom of the oven with foil to catch bacon grease.
2. Place bacon slices on 4-inch rack.
3. Cook on High power (350 degrees F) for 8 minutes. Turn the bacon over and cook for an extra 5 mins or till the bacon reaches desired crispness.
4. Serve straightaway with bread slices and enjoy.

Nutritional Info

- Calories: 541
- Total Fat: 42g
- Total carbs: 1.4g
- Protein: 37 g

Best NuWave Oven Omelet

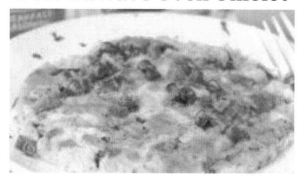

- Ready in 15 minutes
- Servings: 2

Ingredients

- 6 large eggs
- 3 oz. shredded Cheddar cheese
- ¼ c. milk
- ½ c. bacon or ham
- 1/8 c. chopped onion
- 1 medium green pepper, chopped
- ½ tbsp. chopped parsley

Directions

1. In a large mixing bowl combine beaten eggs with milk. Mix using a whisk until the eggs get a fluffy texture.
2. Add the cheese, green pepper, bacon or ham and onion and mix well.
3. Pour the egg mixture in a 4-inch by 4-inch silicon baking dish (grease if you are using a normal baking rack).
4. Put the baking dish on the 1-inch rack. Set temperature on the 'HI' setting and bake for about 10 to 15 minutes.
5. Extract the egg from the silicon-baking dish and slice into pieces.
6. Serve hot with a side dish of baked English muffins or whole wheat bread.

Nutritional Info

- Calories: 194
- Total Fat: 6.9g
- Total carbs: 8.3g
- Protein: 21.7g

Quick & Easy Egg and Bacon Muffins

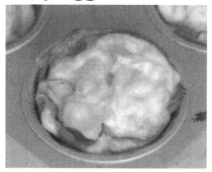

- Ready in 15 minutes
- Servings: 3

Ingredients

- 6 eggs
- ½ c. bacon crumbles
- 1 small onion, chopped
- 1 small red bell pepper, chopped
- 4 tbsp milk
- Salt and black pepper, to taste
- ¼ cup shredded cheddar cheese

Directions

1. Spray 6 cup muffin pot with cooking spray.
2. In a large bowl mix together beaten eggs with bacon crumbles, onion, bell pepper, salt, and pepper. Stir in grated cheese. Mix evenly to combine
3. Spoon mixture into muffin cups. Place muffin pan on 1-inch rack. Cook on High Power (350 degrees F) within 15-20 minutes, till knife inserted in centre of a muffin comes out clear.
4. Serve warm.

Nutritional Info

- Calories: 111
- Total Fat: 8.1g

- Total carbs: 0.6g
- Protein: 8.2g

Cheese Frittata with Basil

- Ready in 30-40 minutes
- Servings: 4

Ingredients

- 1 tbsp. olive oil
- 1 small yellow onion, chopped
- 8 large eggs
- ½ c. milk
- Salt to taste
- ¼ tsp. ground pepper
- 6 oz. sun-dried tomatoes, chopped
- ½ c. goat cheese
- ½ c. basil, chopped

Directions

1. Heat the olive oil in a pan over standard heat and fry the onions until translucent, 3-4 minutes.
2. Meanwhile, in a large mixing bowl whisk together eggs and milk. Season with salt and pepper. Stir in sun-dried tomatoes, goat cheese, basil, and onion.
3. Pour the mixture into the pan. Bake on High power (350 degrees F) for 25-30 minutes, or till toothpick in centre comes out clear. If the top becomes too brown, cover with foil during last stage of cooking.
4. Serve frittata immediately or allow to cool to room temperature. May also be refrigerated for up to 1 day and served cold.

Nutritional Info

- Calories: 146
- Fats: 8g
- Protein: 9g
- Carbs: 11g

English Muffin and Egg Casserole

- Ready in 40 minutes
- Servings: 3

Ingredients

- 12oz. muffins
- 3 large eggs
- 3 slices chopped Canadian bacon
- ¾ c. skimmed milk
- 2 tsp. lemon juice
- 1 tbsp. mayonnaise
- 1 tsp. fresh lemon zest
- Butter

Directions

1. Cut the English muffins into two halves and then chop into 1-inch cubes.
2. In a large mixing bowl combine beaten eggs and milk. Whisk till fluffy.
3. Add chopped Canadian bacon, mayonnaise, fresh lemon juice, and fresh lemon zest to it and mix well until combined.
4. Add the English muffin cubes into the egg mixture and mix till fully coated.
5. Spray a 4-inch by 4-inch baking dish with cooking spray or grease it with butter lightly.
6. Pour the mixture to the prepped baking rack.

7. Place the baking dish on the 1-inch rack. Bake on the 'HI' setting for about 30-40 minutes or until ready
8. Serve and enjoy.

Nutritional Info

- Calories: 367
- Total Fat: 14.6g
- Total carbs: 44.5g
- Protein: 15g

Savory Crab Quiche

- Ready in 20 minutes
- Servings: 4

Ingredients

- 1 Pie crust
- 4 medium eggs
- 1 c. heavy cream
- A pinch of salt
- ¼ tsp. ground black pepper
- 1 tsp. hot sauce
- 1 c. cheese, shredded
- ¼ c. Parmesan cheese, grated
- 1 small yellow onion, chopped
- 2 cans lump crabmeat

Directions

1. Place pie crust on the 1-inch rack and bake on High power (350 degrees) for 6-7 minutes or until brown. Remove from oven and set aside to chill.
2. In a medium bowl, mix eggs, cream, salt, pepper, and hot sauce. Stir in cheeses, onion, and crab meat. Mix well and then transfer the mixture to a pie crust.
3. Place on 1-inch rack and bake on power level High (350 °C) for 15 minutes. Reduce heat to Power level 8 (300 degrees F) and cook for an

additional 10-15 minutes or until a toothpick inserted in centre comes out clear. Allow to relax for 10 minutes before serving.

Nutritional Info

- Calories: 148
- Total Fat: 5.6g
- Total carbs: 14.3g
- Protein: 10.3g

Baked Eggs with Spinach and Tomatoes

- Ready in 15-20 minutes
- Servings: 4

Ingredients

- 8 oz. frozen spinach, chopped
- 3 plum tomatoes, chopped
- 2 garlic cloves, chopped
- ¼ tsp. red pepper flakes
- 8 large eggs
- 2 tbsp. cream
- ½ c. shredded cheddar cheese
- Salt and black pepper, to taste

Directions

1. Cover casserole dish with cooking spray.
2. Squeeze out excess moisture from thawed spinach.
3. Spread tomatoes on the bottom of casserole dish. Lay spinach on top of tomatoes. Season with garlic powder, red pepper flakes, salt, and pepper. Crack eggs on top, drizzle with cream, and sprinkle with cheese.
4. Place dish on 1-inch rack. Bake on High power (350 °C) for 15 minutes or until egg whites are opaque.
5. Serve and enjoy.

Nutritional Info

- Calories: 114
- Fat: 7g
- Carbs: 3g
- Protein: 9g

Mouth-Watering Meat Recipes

Sweet and Spicy Baby Back Ribs

- Ready in 2 hours
- Servings: 4

Ingredients

- 2 tbsp. paprika
- 2 tbsp. granulated onion
- 2 tbsp. granulated garlic
- 1/2 tbsp salt
- 1 tsp cumin
- ¼ tsp black pepper
- 2 tbsp. chipotle or ancho pepper
- 2 tbsp brown sugar
- 6 c. water
- 2 slabs baby back ribs
- 4 tbsp. liquid smoke

Directions

1. In a large bowl combine paprika, onion powder, kosher salt, ground cumin, ground black pepper, chipotle or ancho pepper, garlic powder. Stir to combine well. Add brown sugar to the mixture and stir again.

2. Spoon the prepared spice rub on the slab of baby ribs and coat the baby ribs on all sides. Make sure that you rub the spice rub into all the boney and fatty areas of the baby ribs.
3. Combine the liquid smoke and water together in a mixing bowl. Whisk well until well combined and pour it into the lined pan.
4. Place spice-rubbed baby rib slabs on the 1-inch rack.
5. Set your NuWave oven to the '5' setting and grill your baby ribs for about 90 minutes.
6. Carefully open the lid of the oven, taking care so that you do not burn yourself, and turn the ribs over using metal tongs.
7. Continue grilling the baby ribs for another 3 to 3 and half hours.
8. Once the ribs are done, remove the ribs from oven and rest for 10 minutes.
9. Serve with sauce you prefer.

Nutritional Info

- Calories: 304
- Total Fat: 18g
- Total Carbs: 6g
- Protein: 18g

Rib Roast

- Ready in 30 minutes
- Servings: 3

Ingredients

- 2 lb rib roast
- Salt and freshly ground black pepper, to taste
- ½ tsp. onion powder

Directions

1. In a large bowl combine salt, pepper, and onion powder. Mix well.
2. Put the standing rib roast on the cutting board and sprinkle the prepared rub over the rib roast and rub it in using your hands. Make sure you rub the spice rub in especially around the boney areas.
3. Place the spice rub coated rib roast on a 1-inch rack with its rib side down. Grill on the 'HI' setting for about 14 to 16 minutes per pound of ribs, for rare done ribs.
4. Remove the ribs oven and rest them for about 10 minutes before slicing.
5. Serve hot with hot sauce or barbeque sauce on the side.

Nutritional Info

- Calories: 354
- Total Fat: 25.9g
- Total carbs 0.0 g
- Protein: 28.0

Apple Butter Pork Tenderloin

- Ready in 30 minutes
- Servings: 2

Ingredients

- ¼ tsp. dried thyme
- 1 lb. pork tenderloin
- 1/8 tsp. mustard powder
- 2 garlic cloves, minced
- 4 tbsp. soy sauce
- 4 tbsp. sherry wine

Ingredients for the sauce

- 6 tbsp. apple butter
- 1 tbsp. sherry wine
- 1 tbsp. soy sauce
- ¾ tsp. garlic salt

Directions

1. Combine thyme, garlic, mustard powder, sherry, and soy sauce in a gallon-size zipper-lock bag. Add tenderloin then marinate in the refrigerator for a minimum of 4 hours, preferably overnight.
2. Remove tenderloin from bag, discard marinade, and place in roasting pan.
3. In a large mixing bowl combine the apple butter, sherry, soy sauce, and garlic salt. Cover pork with the apple butter mixture.

4. Place tenderloin on the 4-inch rack and cook on High (350 °C) for 10 - 12 minutes each side.
5. Serve Hot.

Nutritional Info

- Calories: 321
- Total carbs: 9g
- Total Fat: 4.5g
- Protein: 23g

Amazingly Hot and Spicy Chorizo Burgers

- Ready in 20-30 minutes
- Servings: 2

Ingredients

- ¼ lb. chorizo
- ½ tsp. ground cumin
- ¼ lb. lean ground beef
- ¼ tsp. ground coriander
- 2 garlic cloves, chopped
- 1 tbsp. chopped cilantro
- A pinch of salt
- ¼ c. mayonnaise
- Black pepper, to taste
- ¾ tbsp. hot sauce
- 1 tbsp. olive oil
- ½ tsp. fresh lime juice
- 2 slices pepper jack cheese
- Lettuce leaves
- Sliced tomatoes
- 2 hamburger buns
- 1 ripe Hass avocado

Directions

1. In a large mixing bowl place the chorizo, cumin, ½ tablespoon cilantro, salt, beef, coriander, garlic, and pepper.
2. Divide the mixture into two then make 2 patties that are about 3-inches wide and about 1-inch thick each.
3. Place the prepared patties on a 3-inch rack and grill on the 'HI' setting for 8 to 10 minutes on each side.
4. Meanwhile, combine the remaining cilantro with the mayonnaise, lime juice, pepper, hot sauce and salt in a small mixing bowl. Set aside.
5. Once the patties are done and place a slice of cheese on each patty. Continue baking on the 'HI' setting for another minute or until the cheese melts.
6. Spoon the spicy mayonnaise on the bottom buns and place the lettuce, tomato slices and avocado slices on it.
7. Top with the cheese topped burger patties and cover with the top half of the burger bun.
8. Serve hot.

Nutritional Info

- Calories: 334
- Total fat: 23.0g
- Carbs: 1.1g
- Protein: 14.5g

Delicious Honey-Ginger Pork Chops

- Ready in 1 hour
- Servings: 2

Ingredients

- 2 pork chops
- 2 tbsp cider vinegar
- 3 tbsp honey
- 2 garlic cloves, minced
- ½ tsp. ground ginger
- 1 ½ tbsp. soy sauce
- ½ tsp. ground black pepper

Directions

1. In a mixing bowl, add all ingredients apart from pork chops. Stir to combine well.
2. Pour the mixture into large zipper-lock bag and add pork chops. Seal and shake for coating pork chops. Place in refrigerator for a minimum of 1 hour.
3. Place pork chops on 4-inch rack. Cook on High (350 degrees F) for 5 minutes each side or till the pork reaches an internal temp of 160 degrees.
4. Serve and enjoy

Nutritional Info

- Calories: 326

- Total Fat: 5.7g
- Total carbs: 18.4g
- Protein: 19.9g

Barbecue Lamb Skewers

- Ready in 30-40 minutes
- Servings: 2

Ingredients

- 1lb. lamb
- 1 small onion, quartered
- ½ large green bell pepper
- 4 large white mushrooms
- Barbeque sauce
- 2 Roma tomatoes

Directions

1. Divide the lamb cubes, onion quarters and green pepper pieces into two equal portions.
2. Thread the lamb cubes, onion quarters, green pepper pieces, mushrooms and Roma tomatoes on to bamboo or metal skewers in an alternating pattern of meat and vegetables.
3. Place the prepared skewers on the 3-inch rack and lightly brush the barbeque sauce over them.
4. Grill on the high setting for about 12 to 15 minutes.
5. Flip the skewers over and again brush them with the barbeque sauce. Continue grilling for another 8 to 10 minutes.
6. Serve hot with barbeque sauce on the side.

Nutritional Info

- Calories: 287
- Total fat: 12g
- Total carbs: 11g
- Protein: 33g

Spicy Beef Jerky

- Ready in 2 hours
- Servings: 2

Ingredients

- 1 lb. beef steak
- 2 tbsp. soy sauce
- 1 tbsp. Worcestershire sauce
- 1 tsp. liquid smoke
- 1 tbsp. light brown sugar
- Salt to taste
- A pinch of ground black pepper
- ½ tsp. powdered garlic
- ½ tsp. powdered onion
- ½ tsp. cayenne pepper
- ½ tsp. paprika

Directions

1. Place all ingredients in large resalable plastic bag or container with a lid. Mix to evenly coat beef strips. Place in refrigerator and marinate overnight (at least 8 hours).
2. Remove beef strips and arrange in liner pan and 3-inch rack.
3. Cook on Power level 4 (175 degrees F) for 3 to 3 ½ hours.
4. Serve Immediately.

Nutritional Info

- Calories: 189
- Total Fat: 1g
- Carbs: 8g
- Protein: 22g

American Style Pot Roast

- Ready in couple hours
- Servings: 2

Ingredients

- 1 lb. shoulder or chuck roast
- 1 large carrot
- 2 large potatoes
- ½ large onion
- 2 sprigs rosemary
- ¼ cup red wine
- Salt and black pepper, to taste

Directions

1. In a large oven-roasting bag, place the carrots, potatoes and onion together. Place the chuck or shoulder roast over the layer of vegetables.
2. Combine the wine, pepper, salt and rosemary together in a small mixing bowl.
3. Pour the mixture over the meat. Seal the bag with the tie and make a tiny slit on the top.
4. Place the sealed oven-roasting bag on a 1-inch rack with the side with the slit facing up.
5. Set the oven on the '7' setting and roast for about 1-2 hours.
6. Remove the oven-roasting and place on a tray.
7. Give a rest for meat for about 5 minutes before cutting open the bag.

8. Slice the roasted meat and serve hot topped with the cooking jus and with the roasted vegetables on the side.

Nutritional Info

- Calories: 290
- Total Fat: 8g
- Carbs: 37g
- Protein: 18g

Tasty and Easy Lamb Meatballs

- Ready in 30-40 minutes
- Servings: 3

Ingredients

- 1 pound ground lamb
- ¼ tsp. cinnamon
- 2 tbsp. chopped scallions
- ½ tsp. ground cumin
- ½ tsp. salt
- ½ tsp. allspice
- 1 beaten egg
- ½ tbsp. semolina
- 1 tbsp. chopped parsley.

Directions

1. In a large mixing bowl combine the ground lamb and scallions. Mix well.
2. Add cinnamon, allspice, semolina, cumin and salt to the meat and scallion mix. Stir to combine.
3. Pour the beaten egg over the spice-covered meat and use your hands to lightly knead until you get a semi-solid mix. Keep a bowl of cold water handy and constantly wet your palms. This will ensure that the meat doesn't get too sticky to work with.
4. Cover the bowl with a plastic wrap and refrigerate for about an 1 hour or until the meat is firm enough to retain its shape.

5. Divide the meat mixture into 3 parts (about 3 ounces each).
6. Apply oil on your palms and mould each meat portion into a round meatball.
7. Put the meatballs on a 3-inch rack and grill on the 'HI' setting for about 20 to 25 minutes. Pause the oven around the 12-minute mark and turn the meatballs over.
8. Once the meatballs are done, serve hot over a bed of pasta, topped with the sauce of your choice.

Nutritional Info

- Calories: 193.0
- Total Fat: 5.9g
- Total carbs: 4.8g
- Protein: 15.0g

Grilled Steak with Ginger Marinade

- Ready in 30 minutes
- Servings: 4

Ingredients

- Fresh ginger, grated
- 3 tbsp sesame oil
- 4 garlic cloves, minced
- 2 tsp. lemon juice
- 1 tbsp. honey
- A pinch of salt and black pepper
- 1½ lbs. trimmed flank steak

Directions

1. In a medium bowl, whisk all ingredients except steak. Pour into the large resalable plastic bag. Add flank steak, seal, and shake thoroughly to the coat steak with marinade.
2. Allow to marinade for 30 minutes at room temperature. Can also marinate in the refrigerator for up to 24 hours.
3. Remove steak from marinade, allow excess marinade to drip off. Ensure liner is at the base of oven and place steak on the 4-inch rack. Cook steaks on High power until desired doneness, flipping once during cooking.
4. For rare, cook 5-6 minutes per side
5. For medium rare, cook 6-7 minutes each side
6. For medium, cook 7-8 minutes each side

7. For well-done cook 9-10 minutes each side.
8. Insert meat thermometer to check for doneness.
9. Remove from oven and place on chopping board and let rest for 5-10 minutes. Slice, against the grain to thin slices. Serve.

Nutritional Info

- Calories: 215.0
- Total Fat: 11.8g
- Total carbs: 2.9g
- Protein: 23.5g

Savory Poultry Recipes

Amazing Chicken Parmesan

- Ready in 30 minutes
- Servings: 2

Ingredients

- 1 pound chicken breasts
- ½ c. seasoned Panko breadcrumbs
- 2 eggs
- ½ c. flour
- Salt and black pepper to taste
- 14oz. marinara sauce
- 1/2 cup Parmesan, grated

Directions

1. Beat eggs in a shallow bowl and lightly season with salt and pepper. Whisk well.
2. In another shallow bowl put flour and season too.
3. In the third shallow plate place the seasoned panko breadcrumbs.
4. Make light indentions on the chicken breasts with a sharp knife, making sure that you don't cut through.
5. Dip the chicken breasts into the seasoned flour. Then dip the flour coated chicken into the eggs. Finally dip the flour and egg coated

chicken into the plate with the breadcrumbs and lightly press until the breadcrumbs stick to the chicken breasts.

6. Place the breadcrumb encrusted chicken on a 3-inch rack and back on the 'HI' setting for about 15 to 17 minutes per side.
7. Season each slice of chicken with Parmesan and continue baking on the 'HI' setting for another 2 to 3 minutes, or until the cheese melts.
8. Put the chicken breasts on serving plates then slather the marinara sauce over them.

Nutritional Info

- Calories: 254
- Total Fat: 12.38g
- Total carbs: 12.18g
- Protein: 22.83g

NuWave Oven Fried Chicken Wings

- Ready in 25 minutes
- Servings: 3

Ingredients

- 1 ½ lbs. chicken wings
- 1/3 c. grated Parmesan cheese
- 1/3 c. breadcrumbs
- 1/8 tsp. garlic powder
- 1/8 tsp. onion powder
- ¼ c. melted butter
- Salt and black pepper to taste
- Cooking spray

Directions

1. In a baking sheet, spray with cooking spray.
2. In a large bowl mix Parmesan cheese, garlic powder, onion powder, black pepper, breadcrumbs and salt. Stir to combine well.
3. Dip chicken wings one at a time into melted butter and then into bread mixture until thoroughly covered. Arrange wings in single layer on the baking sheet.
4. Place on 1-inch rack and cook on High power (350 degrees F) for 10 minutes. Flip wings over and cook for another 10-12 minutes until no longer pink in centre and juices run clear. Remove promptly from NuWave Oven and serve.

Nutritional Info

- Calories: 371
- Total Fat: 22.6g
- Total carbs: 11.8g
- Protein: 27.8g

Bacon-Wrapped Chicken with Potatoes

- Ready in 28 minutes
- Servings: 4

Ingredients

- 8 slices bacon
- 1 lb. baby red potatoes
- 4 bone-in chicken drumsticks
- 1 tbsp. dried basil
- ½ tbsp. garlic powder
- ½ tbsp. Italian seasoning
- ½ tbsp. black pepper
- 1 tsp. salt

Directions

1. Wrap each piece of chicken with one slice of bacon.
2. Line bottom of NuWave Oven with foil.
3. Arrange chicken in centre of 4-inch rack. Place potatoes around chicken on rack.
4. In medium-sized mixing bowl, combine garlic powder, black pepper, Italian seasoning, basil, and salt. Sprinkle seasoning mixture over chicken and potatoes.
5. Cook on High Power (350 degrees F) for 10 minutes. Turn chicken and potatoes and cook for another 10 minutes or until chicken is fully cooked and potatoes are tender.
6. Serve hot and enjoy.

Nutritional Info

- Calories: 542
- Total Fat: 14.8g
- Total carbs: 74.8g
- Protein: 32 g

Garlic Ginger Chicken Wings

- Ready in 25 minutes
- Servings: 4

Ingredients

- 2 pounds chicken wings
- 1 tbsp. vegetable oil
- A pinch of salt and black pepper
- 1 tbsp. Frank's Red Hot Sauce
- 1/3 c. flour

For glaze

- 3 garlic cloves, minced
- 1 tbsp. Asian chilli pepper sauce
- ¼ c. rice wine vinegar
- 1 tbsp. minced ginger
- ¼ c. light brown sugar
- 1½ tbsp. soy sauce

Directions

1. In a large mixing bowl, combine Frank's Red Hot Sauce, vegetable oil, salt and pepper. Add chicken wings and toss to coat thoroughly.
2. Place coated wings in large zip lock bag. Add flour, seal bag and shake until wings are coated with flour.
3. Place wings on the 4-inch rack and cook on High power (350 degrees F) for 10 minutes. Turn wings over and cook for an additional 8 minutes.

4. Meanwhile, in a large bowl, whisk together all ingredients for glaze. Place wings in glaze and toss to coat evenly. Place wings back on the 4-inch rack and cook on High power for an additional 5 minutes.
5. Remove from oven then serve.

Nutritional Info

- Calories: 312
- Fat: 7.5g
- Carbohydrates: 21.1g
- Protein: 18.8g

Apple-Stuffed Chicken Breast

- Ready in 20 minutes
- Servings: 2

Ingredients

- 2 chicken breasts
- 1 large apple
- 1/4 cup Cheddar cheese, shredded
- 2 tbsp Panko breadcrumbs
- 2 tbsp. Chopped pecans,
- 2 tbsp. Light brown sugar
- 1 tsp. cinnamon
- 1 tsp. curry powder

Directions

1. In a large bowl, add chopped apple, cheese, breadcrumbs, pecans, brown sugar, cinnamon, and curry powder. Stir to combine well.
2. Pound chicken breasts between waxed paper sheets till thick.
3. Spread half the apple mixture on every chicken breast. Roll the chicken up and secure with toothpicks.
4. Place chicken on the 4-inch rack and cook on High power for 12 minutes. Flip over and cook for another 10-12 minutes.
5. Serve Hot.

Nutritional Info

- Calories: 268

- Carbs: 18g
- Fat: 15g
- Protein: 25g

Savory Seafood Recipes

Juicy Citrus Baked Salmon

- Ready in 20 minutes
- Servings: 4

Ingredients

- 4 lemon slices
- 4 orange slices
- 4 salmon fillets
- A pinch of salt and pepper to taste
- 2 tbsp. chopped dill
- 2 tbsp. sun-dried tomatoes
- 1 tbsp. extra-virgin olive oil
- 2/3 c. rice wine vinegar

Directions

1. Place lemon and orange slices, side by side, in the bottom of a shallow baking dish that will fit in NuWave oven (10 x10). Place each salmon fillet across the citrus slices. Sprinkle with pepper and salt.
2. In a large mixing bowl, combine dill, sun-dried tomatoes, olive oil, and rice wine vinegar. Mix well, then drizzle mixture over salmon fillets.
3. Place on 1-inch rack and cook on High power (350 °C) for 7-8 minutes or till salmon is cooked through.
4. Serve and enjoy.

Nutritional Info

- Calories: 270
- Total Fat: 12.6g
- Total carbs: 5.4g
- Protein: 32.5g

Tuna Noodle Casserole

- Ready in 25 minutes
- Servings: 4

Ingredients

- 5 oz. can tuna
- 10½ oz. creamy mushroom soup
- 1 c. egg noodles, cooked
- ¼ c. cold water
- ½ c. frozen peas or green beans
- 2 tbsp. Breadcrumbs
- ¼ c. sour cream
- ½ c. Cheddar cheese, shredded

Directions

1. In a large mixing bowl combine together tuna, sour cream, green beans or peas, about 6 tablespoons cheese, cream of mushroom soup, and cooked noodles.
2. Mix well until it forms a cohesive mixture.
3. Pour the prepared mix into an 8-inch ovenproof dish.
4. Place the ovenproof dish on the 1-inch rack and cook on the 'HI' setting for about 18 to 22 minutes.
5. Once the timer is up, add the remaining cheese and breadcrumbs on the top of the semi-set casserole.
6. Bake on the 'HI' setting for another 2 to 3 minutes or until the cheese melts and gets light brown.

7. Once done, remove the casserole oven and allow cooling for about 7 - 10 minutes before serving.

Nutritional Info

- Calories: 367
- Total Fat: 11g
- Carbs: 25g
- Protein: 19g

Unusual Lime and Tequila Shrimp

- Ready in 25 minutes
- Servings: 2

Ingredients

- 1 pound extra-large shrimp
- 3 tbsp. lime juice
- 2 tbsp olive oil
- 2 garlic cloves, minced
- 2 tbsp tequila
- ½ tsp. ground cumin
- ½ tsp. cayenne pepper
- Salt and ground black pepper to taste

Directions

1. In a large mixing bowl, whisk together lime juice, virgin olive oil, garlic, cumin, cayenne pepper, salt, tequila and pepper. Mix well. Them add shrimps and marinate for 2-3 hours in the refrigerator.
2. Line bottom of NuWave Oven with foil. Place shrimp on the 4-inch rack. Cook on High Power (350 degrees F) for 3 minutes. Flip shrimp over and cook for another 3 minutes or until shrimp are opaque.
3. Serve and enjoy.

Nutritional Info

- Calories: 203
- Total Fat: 5g

- Total Carbs: 6g
- Protein: 19 g

Tender Crab Cakes

- Ready in 35 minutes
- Servings: 3

Ingredients

- 8 oz. lump crabmeat
- 2/3 c. panko breadcrumbs
- 1 tbsp. chopped parsley
- 2 tbsp. chopped green onions
- ½ tsp. Old Bay seasoning
- ½ tsp. Worcestershire sauce
- A pinch of salt
- ¼ tsp. cayenne pepper
- 1tsp. lemon juice
- 2 tbsp. mayonnaise
- 1 large egg
- 1 lemon
- 1 tsp. Dijon mustard

Directions

1. In a large bowl, combine 1/3 cup breadcrumbs, parsley, green onions, Old Bay seasoning, Worcestershire sauce, salt, cayenne pepper, lemon juice, mayonnaise, mustard, and egg. Add crabmeat and stir to combine well.
2. Place remaining breadcrumbs in shallow dish. Form crab mixture into 3 equal size patties. Coat each side with breadcrumbs.

3. Place foil on 3-inch rack. Spray lightly with cooking spray. Place patties on foil. Bake on High Power (350 °C) for 6 minutes. Lip and cook extra 6 minutes.
4. Serve and enjoy!

Nutritional Info

- Calories: 260
- Total Fat: 18g
- Carbs: 13g
- Protein: 11g

Roasted Shrimp with a Herbed Salsa

- Ready in 18 minutes
- Servings: 2

Ingredients

- 1 pound large shrimps
- 3 sliced garlic cloves
- 1 red Serrano pepper
- 1 bay leaf
- ½ lemon
- 3 tbsp olive oil
- Ingredients for the Herb Salsa:
- 2 tbsp. chopped cilantro
- ½ tbsp. grated lemon zest
- 2 tbsp. chopped flat-leaf parsley
- ½ tbsp. virgin olive oil
- Kosher salt and black pepper to taste

Directions

1. Place the shrimp and Serrano pepper halves in an ovenproof dish, along with the bay leaf, garlic and virgin olive oil. Mix lightly till all the ingredients are well coated with virgin olive oil.
2. Place the baking dish on the 3-inch rack.
3. Cook on the 'HI' setting for about 3 to 5 minutes.
4. While the shrimp cooks, prepare the salsa.

5. Combine the cilantro, lemon zest and parsley together in a small mixing bowl. Season with salt and pepper to taste and stir to combine well.
6. Pour the olive oil over the salsa and let it stand for a few minutes before mixing it up.
7. When the shrimp is done, pour in the lemon juice and mix well to coat.
8. Serve the shrimp hot, topped with the prepared salsa.

Nutritional Info

- Calories: 163
- Fat: 3g
- Carbs: 2g
- Protein: 18g

Juicy Vegetable Recipes

Sweet Potato Casserole

- Ready in 15 minutes
- Servings: 4

Ingredients

- 2 c. sweet potatoes
- ¼ c. melted butter
- 1½ tbsp. milk
- ¼ c. honey
- vanilla
- 1 large egg
- ¼ c. brown sugar
- ¼ c. wheat flour
- 2 tbsp. butter
- ½ c. chopped pecans
- Cooking spray

Directions

1. Spray baking sheet with cooking spray.
2. In a large mixing bowl, combine milk, honey, sweet potatoes, vanilla, melted butter, and egg. Mix well.
3. In another mixing bowl, combine brown sugar and flour. Cut in 3 tablespoons butter till crumbly. Add pecans and mix well.

4. Sprinkle the mixture over sweet potatoes.
5. Place on 1-inch rack and cook for 25-30 minutes at 350°C (High) or until golden brown.
6. Serve Immediately.

Nutritional Info

- Calories: 310
- Total Fat: 13g
- Carbs: 49g
- Protein: 3g

Delicious Roasted Garlic Mushrooms

- Ready in 25 minutes
- Servings: 2

Ingredients

- 8 oz. package crimini or button mushrooms
- 2 garlic cloves, minced
- 2 tbsp. olive oil
- 1 tbsp. chopped thyme
- Salt and black pepper to taste

Directions

1. In a medium mixing bowl combine the olive oil, garlic and fresh thyme together. Whisk till well combined. Add pepper and salt to taste.
2. Pour the marinade on the mushrooms and mix well until the mushrooms are properly coated.
3. Place marinated mushrooms directly onto the lined pan.
4. Roast on the 'HI' setting for about 20 to 25 minutes.
5. Serve hot. Enjoy!

Nutritional Info

- Calories: 260
- Total Fat: 18g
- Carbs: 44g
- Protein: 6g

Roasted Cauliflower, Olives and Chickpeas

- Ready in 24 minutes
- Servings: 3

Ingredients

- 3 c. cauliflower florets
- 4 chopped garlic cloves
- ½ c. Spanish green olives
- 15 oz. chickpeas, rinsed and drained
- ¼ tsp crushed red pepper
- 1 ½ tbsp. olive oil
- 1 ½ tbsp. parsley
- Salt to taste

Directions

1. Place the cauliflower florets, garlic, Spanish green olives, chickpeas, crushed red pepper, parsley and salt in a large bowl.
2. Pour oil over the ingredients, then let it stand for about 2 to 3 minutes.
3. Toss until all the ingredients are well coated in the olive oil.
4. Place the olive oil coated ingredients at the bottom of a lined pan in a single even layer. Cook on 'HI' setting for about 22 to 24 minutes.
5. Serve hot with your preferred condiment on the side.

Nutritional Info

- Calories: 176
- Fat: 10.1g

- Protein: 4.2g
- Carbs: 17.6g

Fruit and Vegetable Skewers

- Ready in 20 minutes
- Servings: 4

Ingredients

- 4 tbsp virgin olive oil
- 3 tbsp. lemon juice
- 1 garlic clove, minced
- 2 tbsp. chopped parsley
- ½ tsp. salt
- ½ tsp. black pepper
- 1 sliced zucchini
- 1 sliced yellow squash
- ½ red bell pepper
- ½ c. cherry tomatoes
- ½ c. pineapple chunks
- 4 wooden skewers

Directions

1. In a large mixing bowl combine olive oil, garlic, parsley, lemon juice, pepper, and salt. Pour into large resalable plastic bag. Add zucchini, squash, bell pepper, and tomatoes. Seal bag, shake to coat vegetables, and place in refrigerator for a minimum of 1 hour.
2. Remove vegetables from marinade and thread onto skewers, along with pineapple, alternating among each item.
3. Line bottom of NuWave Oven with foil for easier clean-up.

4. Place skewers on the 4-inch rack. Cook on High Power (350°C) for 8 minutes.
5. Flip skewers over and cook for another 6-8 minutes until veggies are desired level of doneness.
6. Remove from NuWave Oven, transfer to a plate, and serve.

Nutritional Info

- Calories: 173
- Total Fat: 2.8 g
- Total carbs: 36.5g
- Protein: 5g

Roasted Sweet Potatoes with Rosemary

- Ready in 15 minutes
- Servings: 4

Ingredients

- 1 ½ pound sweet potatoes, cubed
- 1 tsp. olive oil
- 1 dash chopped rosemary
- 1 dash lemon juice

Directions

1. In a bowl, toss sweet potatoes with oil. Evenly spread on the 10-inch baking sheet, sprinkle with rosemary. Place on 1-inch rack and back on High power (350 degrees F) for 12 minutes. Flip sweet potatoes over and cook an additional 10 minutes.
2. Drizzle with lemon juice and serve.

Nutritional Info

- Calories: 114
- Total fat: 0g
- Carbs: 27g
- Protein: 2g

Tangy Roasted Broccoli with Garlic

- Ready in 15 minutes
- Servings: 4

Ingredients

- 1 broccoli head
- 3 garlic cloves, minced
- 2 tsp. virgin olive oil
- 1 tsp. sea salt
- ½ tsp. black pepper
- ½ tsp. lemon juice

Directions

1. In a mixing bowl, add oil, salt, garlic and black pepper. Add broccoli. Mix to coat. Evenly scatter broccoli on the 10-inch baking sheet.
2. Place on1-inch rack and roast on High power (350 degrees F) for about 10 minutes. Flip florets and cook another 5-7 minutes or until fork tender.
3. Plate and drizzle lemon juice. Serve at once.

Nutritional Info

- Calories: 141
- Carbs: 10g
- Fat: 10 g
- Protein: 5g

Roasted Carrots with Garlic

- Ready in 20 minutes
- Servings: 2

Ingredients

- 3 tbsp. olive oil
- 2 minced garlic cloves
- Sea salt, to taste
- 1 pound baby carrots

Directions

1. In a medium bowl, mix carrots with olive oil, salt and garlic. Spread carrots in single layer on parchment or foil-lined baking sheet.
2. Place on 1-inch rack and cook on High power (350 F) for 15-20 minutes until carrots are tender.

Nutritional Info

- Calories: 95
- Total Fat: 6.9g
- Total carbs: 7.6g
- Protein: 1g

Savory Roasted Balsamic Vegetables

- Ready in 30 minutes
- Servings: 4

Ingredients

- 1½ c. cubed butternut squash
- 1 c. chopped broccoli florets
- ½ chopped red onion
- 1 chopped zucchini
- 1 minced garlic clove
- 2 tbsp. virgin olive oil
- 1½ tsp. rosemary
- A pinch of salt, to taste
- 1 tbsp. balsamic vinegar

Directions

1. In a mixing bowl, add oil, rosemary, vinegar, pepper, and salt; mix to blend. Mix in the vegetables, mix to coat evenly.
2. Evenly spread on a parchment-lined baking sheet.
3. Place on 1-inch rack and cook on High power (350 degrees F) for about 15 minutes. Flip vegetables and cook for another 15 minutes or until squash is just softened.

Nutritional Info

- Calories: 148
- Total Fat: 4.6g

- Total carbs: 25g
- Protein: 7g

Baked Macaroni and Cheese

- Ready in 25 minutes
- Servings: 4

Ingredients

- ½ pound Cheddar cheese, shredded
- 4 tbsp. butter
- 2 eggs
- 1 tsp. Dijon mustard
- 12 oz. evaporated milk
- 1 pound elbow macaroni
- Salt and black pepper to taste
- ½ c. breadcrumbs

Directions

1. Cook macaroni according to package directions.
2. Spray casserole dish with cooking spray.
3. Add all ingredients except for bread crumbs to a casserole dish and mix well to combine. Sprinkle with breadcrumbs.
4. Cover with foil and place pan on 1-inch rack. Bake on High (350 degrees F) for 15-20 minutes. Remove the foil then cook for another 5-10 minutes or until golden brown.

Nutritional Info

- Calories: 480

- Total Fat: 19g
- Carbs: 31g
- Protein: 24g

Curried Zucchini Chips

- Ready in 24 minutes
- Servings: 2

Ingredients

- 1 medium sliced zucchini
- 1 tbsp. virgin olive oil
- ⅛ tsp. garlic powder
- ¼ tsp. curry powder
- ⅛ tsp. salt

Directions

1. Lightly grease paper-lined baking sheet. Arrange zucchini slices in one layer on the baking sheet. Sprinkle olive oil and dust with curry powder, salt, and garlic powder.
2. Place baking sheet on 1-inch rack and bake on High power (350 degrees F) for 12 minutes. Flip zucchini over and cook for another 10 minutes or till very crisp. Cool and store in airtight container

Nutritional Info

- Calories: 152
- Total carbs: 17g
- Total Fat: 3g
- Protein: 2g

Mouth-Watering Dessert Recipes

Lemon-Zucchini Muffins

- Ready in 30 minutes
- Servings: 6

Ingredients

- 1 c. wheat flour
- 4 tbsp brown sugar
- 1 tbsp. baking powder
- ¼ tsp. sea salt
- 2 tbsp. olive oil
- ¼ tsp. ground cinnamon
- ¼ tsp. nutmeg
- 1 c. shredded zucchini
- ¾ c. nonfat milk
- 1 egg
- 2 tbsp. fresh lemon juice
- Nonstick cooking spray

Directions

1. Prepare 6-muffin tin by spraying with cooking spray or lining with muffin liners.
2. In a large mixing bowl, add flour, baking powder, sugar salt, nutmeg and cinnamon. Mix well.

3. In another mixing bowl, combine milk, zucchini lemon juice, eggs and oil. Mix well.
4. Add zucchini mixture to flour mixture. Stir till just combined. Do not over stir.
5. Pour muffin cups. Place pan on a 1-inch rack and bake for 20 mins at 350 degrees (High) or until light golden brown.

Nutritional Info

- Calories: 371
- Total Fat: 17.5g
- Total carbs: 47.6g
- Protein: 8 g

Baked Stuffed Apples

- Ready in 15 minutes
- Servings: 4

Ingredients

- 4 large apple
- ¼ c. coconut flakes
- ¼ c. dried cranberries or apricots
- 2 tbsp. Grated orange zest
- ½ c. orange juice
- 2 tbsp. brown sugar

Directions

1. Cut top off apple and hollow out centre with knife or apple corer. Arrange in non-stick baking pan.
2. In a large mixing bowl, combine coconut, cranberries, and orange zest. Divide evenly and fill centers of apples.
3. In a bowl, mix orange juice and brown sugar. Pour over apples.
4. Place pan on a 1-inch rack and cook 5-6 minutes until apples are tender.
5. Serve warm.

Nutritional Info

- Calories: 156
- Total Fat: 6.7g
- Total carbs: 26.1g

- Protein: 2g

Carrot Cake Cookies

- Ready in 15 minutes
- Servings: 24 cookies

Ingredients

- ¼ c. brown sugar
- ¼ c. vegetable oil
- ½ tsp. baking soda
- ¼ c. applesauce or fruit puree
- ¼ tsp. nutmeg
- 1 egg
- ½ tsp. vanilla
- ½ c. flour
- ½ c. wheat flour
- ½ tsp. baking powder
- A dash of salt
- ½ tsp. ground cinnamon
- ¼ tsp. ground ginger
- 1 c. old-fashioned rolled oats
- ¾ c. grated carrots
- ½ c. raisins or golden raisins

Directions

1. In a large mixing bowl combine together sugar, oil, applesauce, egg, and vanilla.
2. In another bowl, mix all dry ingredients. Then, add dry ingredients to wet ingredients. Mix till blended. Toss in carrots and raisins.

3. Drop by teaspoonful onto silicone baking ring or parchment-lined cookie sheet.
4. Place on 1-inch rack and cook at 300 degrees F (Level 8) for 12-14 minutes or until golden brown.

Nutritional Info

- Calories: 252
- Carbs: 20g
- Total Fat: 7g
- Protein: 3g

Broiled Peaches with Honey

- Ready in 15 minutes
- Servings: 4

Ingredients

- 2 large peaches
- 1 tbsp. extra-virgin olive oil
- 1 tbsp. honey

Directions

1. Divide peaches in half and eliminate pits.
2. Brush cut side of peaches with olive oil.
3. Put on parchment-lined pan and place on 4-inch rack. Cook in NuWave Oven on High power (350°C) for 5-6 minutes or until peaches are golden brown and caramelized.
4. Drizzle with honey and serve.

Nutritional Info

- Calories: 161
- Fat: 3g
- Protein: 1g
- Carbs: 10g

Dehydrated Cinnamon Apple Chips

- Ready in 2-3 hours
- Servings: 4

Ingredients

- 4 large apples
- 1 tbsp. sugar
- 1 tbsp. cinnamon

Directions

1. Slice off top side (stem) of apples and then slice apples into rounds around 1/8-inch to ¼-inch thick. This is easiest with a mandolin slicer but can also be done with a sharp knife.
2. Place apple slices in a medium bowl and dash with cinnamon and sugar. Mix gently to coat.
3. Spray 4-inch rack with cooking spray. Arrange apple slices on rack.
4. Cook on Power level 3 (150 degrees F) for 4 hours.
5. Remove from NuWave oven immediately. Allow cooling before serving.

Nutritional Info

- Calories: 90
- Total fat: 0g
- Carbs: 26g
- Protein: 1g

Gourmet Honey Cornbread

- Ready in 25 minutes
- Servings: 8

Ingredients

- 1 c. whole wheat flour
- ¼ c. sugar
- 1 c. heavy cream
- 2 tbsp vegetable oil
- 1 c. cornmeal
- ¼ c. honey
- 2 large eggs
- 1 tbsp. baking powder

Directions

1. Grease baking pan lightly.
2. In a large mixing bowl, combine flour, sugar, cornmeal and baking powder. Add in cream, oil, eggs, and honey. Stir to combine.
3. Pour into baking pan. Bake on 1-inch rack on Power Level High (350 degrees F) for 20 minutes. Let rest for 1-2 minutes before removing from NuWave Oven.

Nutritional Info

- Calories: 270
- Total fat: 7g
- Carbs: 26g

- Protein: 3g

Marvelous Chocolate Zucchini Bread

- Ready in 40 minutes
- Servings: 2

Ingredients

- 3 medium eggs
- 1 c. sugar
- 1 c. vegetable oil
- 2 c. grated zucchini
- 1 tsp. vanilla extract
- ¾ c. semisweet chocolate chips
- 1/3 c. cocoa powder
- 2 c. wheat flour
- 1 tsp. baking soda
- A pinch of salt
- 1 tsp. ground cinnamon

Directions

1. Spray two baking pans with cooking spray.
2. In a medium mixing bowl, add, cocoa powder, eggs, oil, grated zucchini, vanilla and sugar. Stir to combine. Fold in flour, baking soda, salt, and cinnamon. Then, add chocolate chips.
3. Pour batter into baking pans. Bake on 1-inch rack on power level High (350°C) for 40-45 minutes until knife inserted in centre comes out clear. Allow bread to rest inside the dome for 1-2 minutes before removing from NuWave Oven. Allow cooling before slicing.

Nutritional Info

- Calories: 217.0
- Total Fat: 8.0g
- Total carbs: 37.0g
- Protein: 3.0g

Pineapple Banana Nut Bread

- Ready in 50 minutes
- Servings: 2

Ingredients

- 3 c. wheat flour
- 3 tbsp vegetable oil
- ¾ tsp. sea salt
- 1 tsp. baking soda
- 8 oz. crushed pineapple
- 2 c. sugar
- 1 tsp. cinnamon
- 1 c. walnuts
- 3 medium eggs
- 4 ripe bananas
- 2 tsp. vanilla extract

Directions

1. Spray baking pans with cooking spray.
2. In a large mixing bowl, add sugar, flour, baking soda, salt and cinnamon.
3. Stir in walnuts, oil, banana, pineapple, eggs and vanilla. Mix till blended. Pour batter to the pans.
4. Place pans on a 1-inch rack and bakes on High power (350°C) for 45-50 minutes or until a toothpick inserted in centre come out clear. Allow

rest under the dome for 1-2 minutes before removing from NuWave Oven. Cool before slicing.

Nutritional Info

- Calories: 216
- Fat: 10g
- Carbohydrate: 30g
- Protein: 3g

Appetizer Blueberry Lemon Cake

- Ready in 45 minutes
- Servings: 1 cake

Ingredients

- 1 tsp. baking powder
- 2 butter sticks
- 1 c. sugar
- ¼ c. fresh lemon juice
- 2 tbsp lemon zest
- 1 tsp. vanilla extract
- 1/8 tsp. salt
- 4 large eggs
- 2 c. wheat flour
- 1½ c. fresh blueberries

Directions

1. Spray the pan with cooking spray.
2. Whisk together butter, sugar, and baking powder until smooth and fluffy. Add lemon juice, lemon zest, vanilla, and salt. Stir to combine
3. Add eggs, one at a time, beating until smooth after each. Add flour and mix until just combined. Fold in blueberries.
4. Spread the batter into the pan. Shake pan to even out the batter.
5. Place Extender Ring on base. Place pan on a 1-inch rack and cook on Power Level 9 (325 degrees F) for 45-50 minutes or until knife inserted in centre comes out clear.

6. Remove from NuWave Oven and allow cooling before slicing.

Nutritional Info

- Calories: 265
- Total Fat: 4.1g
- Total carbs: 52.2g

Useful Cranberry Bars

- Ready in 30 minutes
- Servings: 12 bars

Ingredients

- 1 ½ c. whole cranberries
- ¾ c. white sugar
- ¾ c. water
- 1 package yellow cake mix
- 6 tbsp. melted butter
- 2 eggs
- ¾ c. rolled oats
- 1 tsp. ground ginger
- 1 tsp. ground cinnamon
- ½ c. brown sugar

Directions

1. Spray baking pan with cooking spray.
2. Add cranberries, sugar, and water to saucepan. Cook over medium heat, stirring continuously, until all cranberries pop and mixture thickened for (10-15 minutes). Remove from heat and allow cooling.
3. In a large mixing bowl, add cake mix, butter, brown sugar, oats, ginger, eggs and cinnamon. Spread 2/3 of the mixture into baking pan. Use back of a spoon to press down evenly to form a crust. Spread cranberry mixture evenly over crust. Top with remaining mixture.

4. Place on 1-inch rack and bake on power level High (350 °C) for 30-35 minutes, until top is lightly browned. Allow cooling before cutting.

Nutritional Info

- Calories: 280
- Total Fat: 14g
- Carbs: 38g
- Protein: 3g

Conclusion

I hope you enjoyed the recipes you found on this cookbook. I'm sure you've now found that NuWave Oven is a useful kitchen appliance that can help you prepare a variety of dishes for your family and friends. Cook delicious breakfasts, juicy meat and poultry dishes, savory seafood, vegetables, and incredible desserts. Thanks to the newest technologies, all your dishes are cooked quickly, they are tasty and useful.

In conclusion, I would like to say Thank You again for buying my cookbook. I am sure that you will return to it again and again in search of tasty and favorite recipes.

Made in the USA
Columbia, SC
18 May 2020